CITADELS

CITADELS

JEANINE STEVENS

Folded Word
Meredith, New Hampshire

ISBN: 978-1-61019-119-7

Folded Word
79 Tracy Way
Meredith, NH 03253
United States of America
www.foldedword.com

Author portrait by Greg Chalpin

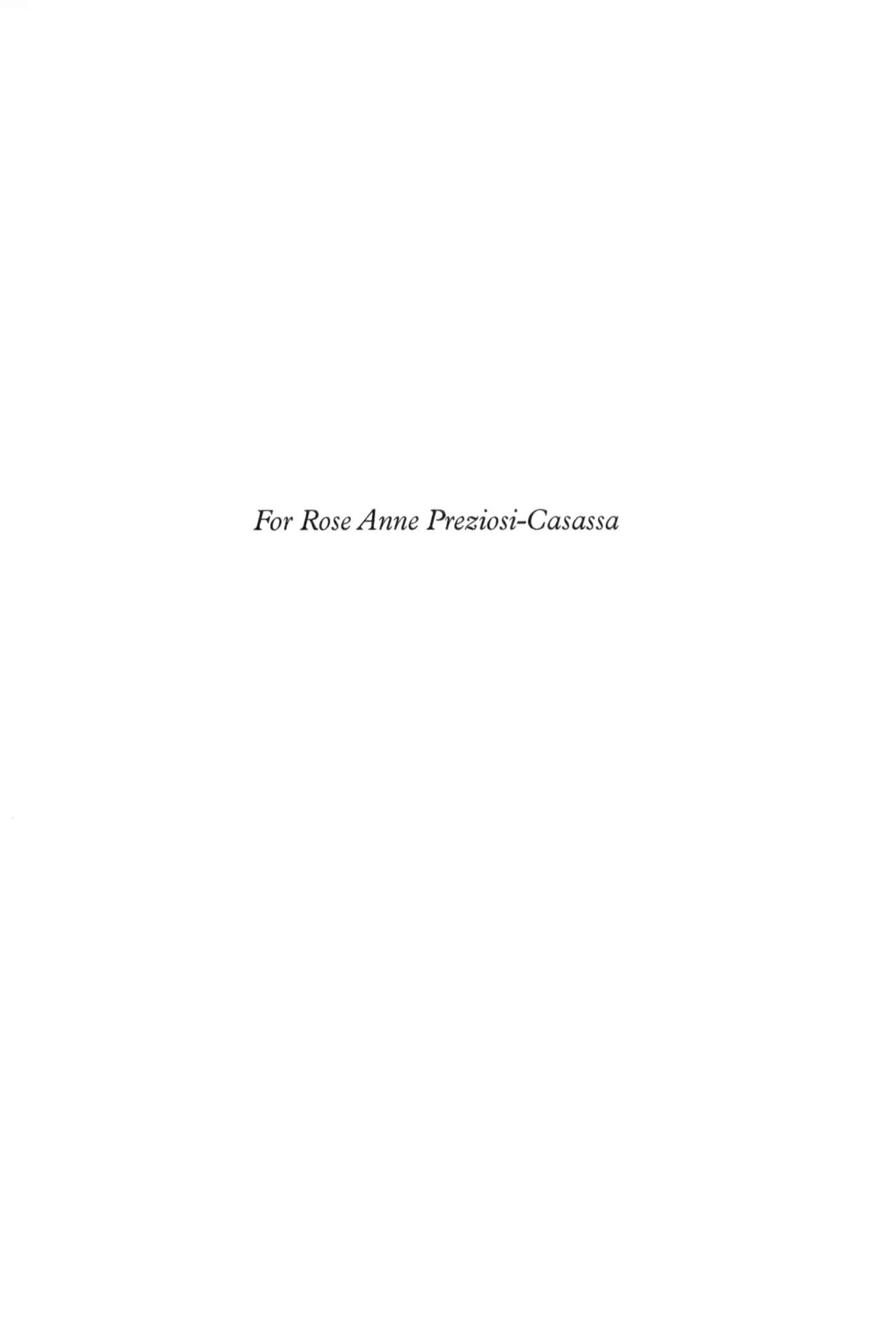

For Rose Anne Preziosi-Casassa

CONTENTS

Acknowledgements

Grateful acknowledgements to the editors of the following publications in which these poems first appeared, sometimes in earlier versions.

Blue Fifth Review, "Italian Summer"
Clackamas Literary Review, "False Pilgrim"
Colere, "At the Uffizi" and "Cento Italia"
Dragonheart, "Chapel in the Snow"
Forge Poetry Journal, "Vinci in Winter" and "Tree of Wooden Clogs"
Found Poetry Review, "Lights Out New York"
Medusas' Kitchen, "Lighthouse"
North Dakota Review, "The Bridge to Civitá di Bagnoregio"
Poetry Now, "Sea Gulls in Bath"
Poet's Espresso, "I Dream of Water"
Poppy Road, "Canterbury"
Raven's Perch, "January in the Vineyards"
The Gathering, "Prufrock in Venice"

The Ghazal Page, "Unhinged"
The MacGuffin, "Watching Hummingbirds
with Sun Tzu"
Turtle Island Quarterly, "Minimums"
Verse Wisconsin, "Street Scene in Venice"

Thank you to JS Graustein for selecting *Citadels* and guiding the manuscript through all phases of production. Also to Greg Chalpin for the beautiful cover photo of Civitá di Bagnoregio.

Much appreciation to the Italian Cultural Society, Sacramento, for the enriching Thanksgiving week in Tuscany and to Jim Luotto and Diane Macario for their assistance with the manuscript and for making our time in Montefiascone so memorable.

~ Jeanine Stevens
April 2019

No book is possible without the people of its press. The author and publisher would like to thank Rose Auslander, Zakariah Johnson, Casey Tingle, Sarah Gibson, Barbara Flaherty, Kristine Slentz, Tobi Carter, Heidi Marshall, and Claire Graustein for their assistance at the press during the production of this book.

CITADELS

False Pilgrim

My feet are not quantum
nor measured in brown:
boxes, toggles and bones.

I want more than tossing stones
like vagabond shoes, or something
wild, like snakes on Mars.

Wren catches fortune
in her throat, disturbs
and scatters cold wind.

The arena fills with winter rains.
Each clasp repairs, latches
bronze with clean and shine.

The hastened trek brought me   here
my cancelled check keeps me   near.

The borders of Rome never were,
calculations made in error,
turn around, shoot the arrow.

Street Scene

All humans stream at night…
into the loving nowhere.
~ *Rumi*

Late on Sunday, we unpack our bags,
locate the A/C switch, then walk the Grand Canal,
search for a place to eat and have
some local wine.

The breeze off the water smells of lime trees.
In Venice, we are in no hurry.
The fish market closes,
a few stalls hold discarded items:
rusty kerosene lantern
and a busted orange crate stamped *Valencia*.

A clay pot catches my eye,
one handle missing, decorated with mud-frogs
and delicate plants, things
that would thrive in a lily pond.
I want to take it home but your knee stiffens.

In a fuchsia sunset, we drink our wine
near the Rialto Bridge.
That night, I dream of an altar somewhere
near the Aegean, perhaps the west coast of Turkey.
On a turquoise fresco, a woman watches
a man gazing down at her.
He whispers of strange flowers,
rare amphibians and waters gurgling
cool and fresh from icy streams.

Italian Summer

We take the long walk
to the Guggenheim
and enjoy an air conditioned lunch.

Later, *Prosécco* on the square,
and jazz quartets in white tuxedos.

In St. Mark's, carpets are thrown
over tiles for safety; the force
of even a gentle wake
upends delicate mosaics.

In the dark grandeur here
and the frescos in the Doge's Palace,
I expect tears. But it's a glance

to the east that smarts my eye.
Rose-colored structures on near islands,
shimmering in the Adriatic's blue water,

dwarfed and broken
by a sparkling cruise ship,
like a white wolf, wet nose poking

in the chicken coop, slathering, soundless,
yet causing uproar, spewing heavy
surf on worn and fragile walkways,

the convenience of tourism breaking
away irreplaceable ground.

I wonder at this tender strip of land,
begin to understand Shakespeare,

why the merchant's daughter
could simply slip away unnoticed
with all the family's gold.

Prufrock in Venice

No one will take our photo in the piazza
as we enjoy a strong espresso

or leave the cathedral
trying to decide if we should risk
a boat ride to the island.

We try not to look like tourists
but your shirt, a blue line print on parchment
with its ancient map of the world, draws stares.

We are not royalty, no one expects
anything from us.

We purchase toy gondolas for the holiday
tree we haven't put up in years.

The city moves. We can hear
floorboards meet, that gentle grind and squeak.

Our suitcase wears thin.
The zipper loses stitching.
The duct tape inside might show —
what if we're searched?

Better to die, even drown near famous museums,
and not know the embarrassment.

We do enjoy the Chianti and small pastries.
We do love the pink peaches reflecting dawn.

At the Uffizi

In the Renaissance exhibit,
so many Madonnas,
grand birthings, effluence.

In gold gilt frames,
uniform robes in crimson and blue,
the Marys look at the child
who looks away.

In a more modern gallery,
framed in distressed wood,
                they boldly stare.

Now, in gray homespun,
they never grasp or hold
                the child tight.

In one painting, the boy looks up,
has questions and seems as if
he might fall.

And where are the *putti* —
those protective toddlers
with angel wings?

In the background, bent thorn trees
twist and hover near
red-veined leaves and spotted ivy.

Florence 2009

Relic

Summer, when kids are out of school.
I should have known better.
Still, I volunteer to ride in the gondola
with six teens, their own stories
drowned out by an accordion playing,
  "O Sole Mio."
Near sundown, the blues
and purples of the Grand Canal dig deeper.

Then Florence, and a visit to the Galileo exhibit.
In one display, a single finger encased
in a glass egg. Did this finger hold a pen, fasten
a buckle, tweak the flame on a candle?

The card says, *spernas digiti,*
and questions, “Is the finger pointing
to the universe or to his oppressors?”

I think, why not both?
And I remember the finger puppets
crafted so many years ago for my own children —
soldier, bear and monkey
still tucked away in my closet,
no longer in use, not really toys at all.

The teen who wears a T-shirt that says
Spoiled and Ready has been boisterous,
even belligerent. He stands next
to me and Galileo's fragment, then
sits on a bench, hands folded in his lap,
hardly speaks for the remainder of the trip.

Cento Italia

The sun drinks up stones
bleached white.

In the distance, the song
of silk looms, slowly spent.

This morning I lay
down in an urn of water
and like a relic
rested there.

I crouched
near my clothes
soiled with war
and like a Bedouin
I bowed to receive the sun.

Bellagio with lifted ears,
flowers quivered,
flowers curled
in sleep.

On a sea yellow,
limpid fresh and electric
was the light of evening.

~Aldo Palazzeschi, "The Palatine"
and "Voyage to Montevedo"

~ Guiseppe Ungaretti, "Rivers"

Unhinged

~A Ghazal

On the train to Rome, cigar smoke clouds my
window;
people eat mortadella and a porter sells gum and
mints.

I travel to a sacred place, discover a broken latch.
In prayers of my own device, I have questions.

We know that image, fluid and ever-changing.
For hysterics, pause — take a whiff of valerian.

This story spins in the night, this tale one
of a limping dog drinking fetid water. I'm unhinged
   by stars.

Seaweed bends to the pressure of water. In my
pea-green boat, I sail down to the purpling ocean.

A woman carries a milk jug, a flute plays under a
banyan tree. Returning, nothing will look the same.

Tree of Wooden Clogs

~ Film, Ermanno Olmi, Italy, 1978

The tenant farmer amid rain, mud
and chicken droppings,
sacrifices, buys school books for his son,
the brightest, who lights up every detail.

The winter is wet and harsh.
The walk long, the boy arrives home late.
Rain and frost crack and split
his thin shoe. A graceful row of trees.
One is chopped,
carved into a pair of small clogs.

Driving a new roadster,
the landowner stops
by the downed pine, demands the culprit,
expels the family from the compound,
so much cut down along this country road.

Viewing again in 2012, I hear
the beautiful Bergamasque dialect
and now recognize Bach's fugue,
a soundtrack so necessary for flight.

Vinci in Winter

In this small village, chilled by late November rain,
sweetness comes from hillsides puffed with sheep.

I climb past beryl-tinted groves to the family home,
a middle class dwelling, perhaps grander in its day.

I see a small boy on fluffy carpets sketching
before the orange-tongued hearth.

A domed ceiling welcomes diffused light,
scant shadows on plaster walls, the fire

sparking images starker than the pale sun.
Did he listen to the farm cart's rattle on stone,

repetitive motion, or from a window,
note gushing streams and iron watersheds?

Look into the stains of walls, or ashes of a fire
or mud; you may find marvelous ideas.

On leaving, I see birds scan small rodents,
wait for brash thermals, the center bone of flight.

Trees drench sieved textures like lush swatches
clipped from velvet bolts, crushed sage and violet.

Twisted trunks seem screwed to earth, black olives
saved for oil, still cling. How warmed I am.

The beauty of fret-worked roads,
a matter of years, no shortcut to genius.

~ *Italics: from Da Vinci's Notebooks*

Chapel in the Snow

On this bright pinnacle, Etruscans found paradise:
emerald lush, white seeking white.
Others came with heralds, symbols
and built this Pope's sanctuary. Storms caved
the roof, leaving Mary's portrait in the snow.

Today the scent of rosemary springs loose
from creviced walls. A row of hollyhocks, ivory petals
translucent as butterfly wings, graze my hand,
    lead me to the chapel.
Inside, saints in frescos, golden clips
in bronzed hair, seem to leap skyward, pleading,
    "Do not forget us."

Changing light creases the row of violet cypress,
branches reach like fingered shadows toward the
    Rocca.
Sun plants shimmer splotches,
like mercurial coins.

Lovers know this as blessing,
fall in love all over again.

A whisper travels from the lake, *Stay!*
Like a soft lullaby,
everything gold folds: halos, pigment, and vessels
holding frankincense.

From the belvedere, I watch the setting
sun lay satin ribbons on the water; the chapel
glistens.
Falling snow can make any roof a temple.

At St. Maria in Castello
Montefiascone 2009

**Rocca: an ancient fortress*

January in the Vineyards

Afternoon at the Villa Toscano,
a winter white sky and partial sun.
Miles of deciduous vines, black and angular.
Patches of snow remain in blue shade.

A sudden influx of cream-colored sheep nibble
green tufts near the living base,
earth still breathing,
small teeth tugging at sleeping roots.

Almost a monochrome print one would find
in a metropolitan home: tuxedo and pearl.
Except the sheep are more like the fluffed shade
of boiled-wool jackets, Chanel style, ones
you might find at a vintage street market

Nights begin early. At the hearth, fire cracks
amber stars, poems read more slowly.
Fog settles between the houses,
sheep and vines bed down to warm earth.

Minimums

On the bluff above the river, the puffy owl sleeps
secure
in his round hole. Blue oaks denote a change in
elevation

and somewhere, a flock of five pointed stars exist
just as I have imagined. In human thought there are
no

minimums. What seems a void is rapidly filled like
soft air
packed in Vermeer's porcelain pitcher. Always, a
decision:

shorten the fugue, omit the tree from the pencil
sketch, take
the elbow out of the poem, the raisins from the
pudding.

The ax handle explains the history of tools. Fossil
grains
prove the origin of beans. Even haiku gives us an
entire season.

In the hush of convent and cell, the mind dreams on
the wall,
and a slim finger traces our moonlit history in a
single night.

BACCHANALIA

~ Picasso, Linoleum Cut

White clouds as blurbs
hastily written
hoot the moon.

Two fleshy dancers
stride akimbo
orange feet planted
like penny kangaroos.

A retired trombone player
toots the jazziest of tunes.

The ebony bull on the dais
sports an anxious hunch, waits
his turn to bellow.

Shaking maracas X-out
the wind, revise old-time lyrics
spell out…a very blue
a very milky… Moo!

The Bridge to Civitá di Bagnoregio

On the caldera, a donkey treks the narrow path,
supplies in a wicker basket.
The postcard, a black and white photo
circa 1943 just after the bombing,
shows edges blown away,
the railing near collapse.
The caption reads,
An eternal cycle of settlement,
abandonment, re-habitation.
Built by Etruscan dust and blood, Civitá
shimmers in the noonday sun.
In the high piazza, flowerpots hug
entries to small shops.
A merchant offers olive oil tasting,
tables, candles, soft music from a tape recorder.
He says tourism is down, the city's again
in trouble. Still, there is something
permanent, celestial, about the deep blue air,
the cascading red-orange geraniums.

On the walk back, a cacophony of songbirds,
invisible in a deep valley, melodies
enfolding, one *canzonette* after another.
I look down to this fluffy ceiling, birds surely
moving in a pink mist that anoints
this grand congregation, this most ancient grove.
It seems an endless cycle of mirth,
    chee-chee, chee-chee,
piping whistles, high-pitched whinnies,
perhaps the linnet, haw finch, or day owl,
a warbling broadcasts the wonder of merry hearts.
Giacomo says, "I have never heard
    their songs so melodious."
Motorized carts have replaced the faithful donkey.
Time here is not linear, not my time,
with docks, rivers and ports of call as proof.
Civitá is tender, a place where transitory events
simply rest on the surface.
This may be the closest I come to Eden.

Lighthouse

Abandoned, it watches oncoming clouds,
a darkening lens,
soot splashing night.

Rungs are missing from the ladder,
remaining ones splintered.

Where is the keeper
drawn close to the pellet stove
warming worn hands?

I think of Venice,
where I spent yellow days looking
for Geppetto and Jessica,
the dreamy Adriatic glittering
mauve and emerald.

But, this is Oregon.
I hope between storms, the air clears
just enough for a glimpse —
the lime-green flash at sunset.

I Dream of Water

You crossed the bridge
to buy picnic supplies.

Turbulent water flooded
the levee, broke that bridge
  and the next.

But, downstream, others held.
I thought I saw you

on the frontage road eating
a sandwich, looking, but not

seeing. It took water
  to move you?

Dark again! I wait

another evening
  writing this reverse aubade.

Watching Hummingbirds with Sun Tzu

Even in drought years they return to each bower
seeking milkweed, bog sage and brilliant cone
flower,

then hover, blurred velocity dispersing mist,
mechanical whirligigs rearranging winter's dust.

A furious twirling, Chopin's *Minute Waltz* playing,
wing-shear warping white air, sweet roses fraying.

And in breeding season, boundaries soon plucked,
fiery gorgets alert, eyes penetrating a sullen roost.

One completes a pendulum swing, squeaky voice
grating,
chick chick, chick chick, such a boisterous mating.

Another flies backward, sketching an aerial eclipse,
a grand reconnaissance, a shrilling, *vrrp vrrp, vrrp vrrp...*

Watching with Sun Tzu, we agree these diminutive wardens
know a good thing; all covet that same primordial garden.

Mid-afternoon. In a glass jar, remnants of fragrant Sun Tea.
I wonder about thresholds, the original Eden, the elusive sea.

Lights Out: New York

~ 21st Century Initiative

"Turn off upper-story lights by midnight
during migrations along the Atlantic Flyway."
Artificial lighting disrupts a bird's innate
navigation system, killing or injuring.

I remember those wings,
innumerable chevrons whooshing
behind dusky windows. I remember
yellowish sulfuric stars and planets

on my childhood ceiling,
my fears distracted for a moment
until sirens blared.

My aunt stood on top of the Crown Plaza
"plane spotting." The aging air-warden
patrolled the street, notepad in hand,
hoping for infractions.

I nervously held a candle
under three blankets, watched my baby sister
gasp from whooping cough, fighting
for breath, the weak flame crackling my hair.

Yet tonight, a new century, this flyway,
at least, is clear and open so white-throated sparrows
and ruby-crowned kinglets are safe from even
the tiniest beams now banned by night.

CANTERBURY

Wind blows stiff from the White Cliffs.
Along the road, rape seed fields pulse
florescent, like Van Gogh's
colors in his warm weather mania.
First I visit the cloisters
protected from swift gusts,
then downstairs to the shadowy,
11th century crypt and sullen dust,
a place for quiet, prayer, and reflection.

I brought my travelers lamp (really just
a tiny book light from Blackwell's).
On the carvings I read some good history
and some bad. Of a sudden, walls
reverberate, earth heaves,
sound lodges in my bones.
A quake? No, darker,
like a rumbling night mission.

Is it because I'm here with no real intent?
Someone gives a small cry.
I hurry upstairs to the light —
a vast choir on temporary bleachers
rehearses the Verdi "Requiem."

V-E Day, 2015

Citadels

Usually in summer, snow remains
in the cross-shaped crevice near the summit,
but in this drought year — only a dark indent.

Walking at the shrinking shoreline,
vacationers arrange temporary edifices:
a heart embedded in a lover's knot,
a miniature fortress, its bulwarks
studded with fresh-water clams and three
small turrets hoisting a single goose feather.

I wade further out; toes grip tough ripples
in the sand. Abstract spirals coil
in grey granite. It seems these tiny monuments
are signs of shipwreck, a string of SOS
messages for a thirsty, damaged,
but still beautiful planet and I have stumbled

across the ancients, their meanings in shapes,
before unhewn stone, before struck flint,
temporary reminders we are all just borrowers.

I walk to the west. Sun glosses over the mountains.
In the tangerine glow, an old man and woman
construct a pinecone labyrinth.

Outside the boathouse, I listen as the Scottish
fiddler
plays old tunes from the Shetland Islands.

Lake Tahoe 2015

Sea Gulls in Bath

At *Aquae Sulis*, Roman generals hold silent court.
Green waters ripple old melodies on lute strings.

August heat demands open windows, eight sleepless
hours traded for a few brief breezes. Herring gulls

perch on every sill: gold-rimmed lids, light yellow
irises like tiny spinning suns, gawk as if humans

had just arrived in England. They rampage
ear-creasing, high-pitched squawks — *kyow* and
hyah,

longer notes far beyond measured decibels. Bird
noise seems to taunt moonlit statues. Silver spires

of Bath Abbey dwarf the largest commander who
gazes inward, melting dreams in submerged pools,

so far from home. Across the River Avon, a stone
labyrinth; I walk to the center, cannot find my

way out. A child comes to my rescue and leads me
— worm trails and hexagons slither and gleam.

Compline

Evening comes
with all the finished hours.
In Tai Chi, I find the needle in the sea
where the white snake creeps down.

Evening comes with all
the finished hours. Late coffee at La Bou,
a fifth re-vision of my Milwaukee poem.

Evening comes, the
finished hours, evening meal: salmon,
greens, the Colbert Report with logo:
a screeching eagle I learn is actually a hawk.

Evening comes. I finish
reading the book about a burial,
an unwed mother faces West,
her fetus faces East.

Evening. A moongarten
leaks under redwood trees, twin skunks
dance a nocturne at midnight.

fin

About the Author

Jeanine Stevens is the author of *Limberlost* and *Inheritor* (Future Cycle Press), and *Sailing on Milkweed* (Cherry Grove Collections). *Brief Immensity* recently won the Finishing Line Press Open Chapbook Award. Other prizes include the MacGuffin Poet Hunt, the Stockton Arts Commission Award, the Ekphrasis Prize, Mendocino Coast Writer's Conference Award, and WOMR Cape Cod Community Radio National Poetry Award. She was one of two finalists for the William Stafford Award. Poems have appeared in the *Curator*, *Evansville Review*, *North Dakota Quarterly*, *Chiron Review*, *Forge*, *Pearl*, *Stoneboat*, *Connecticut River Review*, *Provincetown Magazine* and *Rosebud.* Jeanine recently received her sixth Pushcart Nomination. She is a member of the Community of Writers at Squaw Valley and has worked with Sharon Olds, Forrest Gander, Robert Haas and Brenda Hillman. She studied poetry at U.C. Davis and California State University, Sacramento, and has graduate degrees in Anthropology and Education. Jeanine also enjoys collage, and her work has been exhibited at Red Dot Gallery, Dada Gallery, and Sparrow Gallery. Jeanine is Professor Emeritus at American River College, having taught for thirty-two years in Anthropology, Psychology and Women's Studies. Raised in Indiana, she now divides her time between Sacramento and Lake Tahoe, California.

About the Press

Since 2008, Folded Word has been
exploring the world, one voice at a time
with the help of editors, authors, and readers
who value sustainable literature.

For a complete list of our titles, visit the Folded Word website: FOLDED.WORDPRESS.COM

To report typographical errors, email:
FoldedEditors@gmail.com

Want more information about our titles? Want to connect to our authors? No problem. Simply join us at a social media outlet near you:

Facebook: FACEBOOK.COM/FOLDEDWORD
Twitter: TWITTER.COM/FOLDEDWORD
Instagram: INSTAGRAM.COM/FOLDEDWORD

FOLDED WORD

is a proud member of

[clmp]

Community of Literary Magazines and Presses

Ensuring a vibrant, diverse literary landscape

WWW.CLMP.ORG

and gives annual support to:

Poets House

A place for poetry: library, literary center, locus of poetic inspiration

WWW.POETSHOUSE.ORG

The Haiku Foundation

Preserving and archiving the first century of haiku in English; providing resources for the next

WWW.THEHAIKUFOUNDATION.ORG

What did you think?

Let us know with a quick rating at
www.GoodReads.com
or wherever you search for books.

Folded Word reserves a portion of each print run to donate to libraries and reading programs in under-served communities. Please email us at FoldedEditors@gmail.com if you would like your organization to be considered.

Colophon

Cover and textblock design by JS Graustein, featuring the photograph "Civitá di Bagnoregio" by Greg Chalpin.

The title face is Core Deco, designed by Hyun-Seung Lee, Dae-Hoon Hahm, and Minjoo Ham, issued by S-Core in 2014.

The accent face is DrSugiyama Pro, designed by Alejandro Paul from an original face by Charles Bluemlein, issued by Sudtipos in 2009.

The text face is Plantin Pro, designed by Frank Hinman Pierpont, issued by Monotype in 2001.